Feeding Wild Birds

Feeding Wild Birds

Poems by Robert Haight

Mayapple Press 2013

Published by   MAYAPPLE PRESS
                362 Chestnut Hill Rd.
                Woodstock, NY 12498
                www.mayapplepress.com

ISBN 978-1-936419-27-2

ACKNOWLEDGMENTS

Thanks to the editors of the following publications in which versions of these poems first appeared:

Ambassador Poetry Project: Six A.M.; *Angel Face:* Assimilation; *Bluestem:* To a Coyote; *California Quarterly:* Mother After the Stroke; *Cortland Review:* A Beautiful Snowy Day, Late Fall, Walking, Winter Night; *Driftwood:* The Servant of Small Things, The Man I Would Become; *Encore*: Eliane Elias Plays Jobim; *Karamu:* Another Morning; *The Michigan Poet*: In February; *Passages North:* The Danger of Poetry; *White Pelican Review:* Lectio Divina @ Amazon.com.

"The Danger of Poetry" was reprinted in *Passages North Anthology*, Milkweed Editions. "Mother After the Stroke" was reprinted in a limited edition of *Driftwood*. "Man in Float Tube" appeared in the exhibition "Second Sight/Insight" at the Kalamazoo Institute of Arts. "Let Snow Fall" originally appeared on the websites of Poets Against the War and Kalamazoo Non-violent Opponents of War. "Walnuts in Winter" is dedicated to Gordon Bielby.

Many thanks to Keith Kroll, Rod Torreson and Margaret von Steinen for their friendship, advice and support of this writing.

Cover photo and cover design by Judith Kerman. Book designed and typeset by Amee Schmidt with titles and text in Calisto MT.

Contents

III

IV

For Rob and Santana
and for Tomasa, always

Bright moon in pines. By their doors peace.
Sunrise. From clouds the wild birds call.

—*Wang Wei*

Planning a Poem

When I take the dogs
out for their walk just after dawn

I might intend to notice
how many more leaves have fallen
in the breeze onto Maple Road since yesterday

as summer makes its slow September
turn toward autumn

or I might check how many more leaves
on the birch have become gold coins
while most still wear green

or see how the bean field down the road
bleached by the sun another afternoon
has lightened to a new shade of amber

until I approach the ponds
where a heron that must have spent the night
standing as still as driftwood on the shore

unfurls and flaps the blue sheets
of its wings and lifts off into the air.

Three Days in March

*You do not call winter the beginning of spring, nor summer the
end of spring.*
                                    —Dogen

i.

Early March. Tinfoil sky.
Snow dust swirls over the field
        of broken cornstalks.

Yesterday, twenty geese
        became a single
pair of wings.

        Today they have disappeared,
perhaps deep in the swamp
where a certain angle of sunlight

in the empty weekday afternoon
brings songbirds to the bare trees
        their claws scratching the branches into leaf.

ii.

First rain of spring
a washboard sky scrubs the stubble field
        once waves in wind before the harvesting

now by the faint sea light of stars
        a south wind brushes the budding trees
in the muted air before dawn

        it can't be held, this thaw, this melting
that forms morning behind the limbs
the swamp filling with songs

as lake ice darkens and disappears
a swan settles on the water
        floating snow sculpture

iii.

After so many days of rain, the sun.
Flowers can't keep their eyes off it.
        Their heads follow it across morning

and through the afternoon.
        Robins dig and sip rain-wet grass.
They sing again after days of the song

        that washed the paper wasps from the eaves.
We begin to accept the plausibility of splendor
that coveted spring light.

Mother After the Stroke

Your thoughts have become butterflies
that light for a moment to twitch their wings
then lift off into air again

as you begin a sentence
and stop after a few words
looking around to see which direction
the idea might have flown.

There is a grace in this,
the plank by plank construction
of your personality
left in a heap after the storm,
the bigotry and suspicion
that once housed you
softening to its pulpy conclusion

leaving you exactly where you are,
smiling to everyone who passes.
They are all your friends now,
all so beautifully human to you,
the words you can no longer cage
fluttering around you.

Picture I.D. of My Father

There you are in that photograph
on the last driver's license I found
among your papers and cuff links
in an old box in the back of the closet.
You wear a half-smile, having made it
over to the Secretary of State's office
and having passed the vision test.
The other half, the smile that is missing,
knows this was a labor far beyond
a minor item on an errand list,
that for days you put it off thinking
you would fail, that another indignity
of aging and declining health would
be visited upon you in public, under the glare
of fluorescent lights, the strangers all looking
at you as they shuffle in line waiting to renew
their licenses or registrations.
Your white hair is longer than I ever
remember it before you retired.
It is sticking up wildly as if you were
some philosophy professor instead
of the businessman in a suit you prepared
to become each morning for so many years.
This day you are wearing a flannel shirt
as if you're on your way up north
to fish, though I know from the look
in your eyes you would never even try,
that the line would get tangled
into a confused nest you could never make
sense of, that you could never pull apart.

The Danger of Poetry

This poem takes place in another country
and if that country is Canada
it takes place in Quebec, though one might

prefer Mexico of those countries bordering us
on aesthetic grounds and it may as well
take place somewhere else. It is a poem

about my father, who came from Canada
though that was when he was just a boy.
Since the poem is from my memory

I will be in another country
though I haven't traveled out of the U.S.
since a trip to Jamaica five years ago

which, by the way, would make a perfect setting
for this poem, unless it is already taking place
in Mexico or Quebec.

I am remembering my father coming home
from the plant, metal shavings sticking
from his torn hands. In reality he was a purchasing

agent for a chain of movie theaters, but in that case
his hands would not stick metal shavings.
Anyway, he gets home and we dance

in the kitchen, my stocking feet on top
of his work boots, though he really wore wingtips,
my ear scraping against the belt buckle.

There must be a bottle of whiskey somewhere
in this poem—yes, there it is over there
on the cutting board, a fifth of Jack Daniels

Black Label which is filled only to the – on the No. 7.
The remainder of the whiskey I will place
on his breath, though in truth my father was a strict

scotch man. After dancing awhile he scoots me
off to bed, and on the way upstairs I tell him
how stubborn he is and how much I hate him.

For twenty years after that I travel around
waiting for that time when we will meet and make
our peace, which is why this poem is taking place

in Jamaica or Mexico or Quebec in Canada where I
very likely have been studying something esoteric
my father has no use for. But, of course, this too

is not true. None of this is true.
This is the danger of poetry:
what it will get you to do for more.

14

The Man I Would Become

I shadow him like a child
pushing a plastic mower
along strips of fresh-cut lawn
following his father

and I am right behind him
when he strides into the darkness of three a.m.
to check an unlocked window
or open barn door.

I stand silent as he holds his gaze
on the eyes of the razor-wielding punk
and tells him to go home
and look for work.

Now I still can see him
a day, month, year in the future
on his knees to help an old lady
who spilled her groceries

while when I turn to look behind me
I see through the window
the man I once was
sitting at the bar of the past
sipping from a frosted mug of beer
and drawing from his smoke
content to spend the entire day inside
reminiscing.

Crossing the Rapids on a Twenty Degree Morning in March

Stone by stone
spray of cobble

soft indentation
of sand

between boulders
that could cut

a person down
at the shins

not the destination
but the journey

no long strides
steps like first kisses

sharp-edged granite
sunken branches

stabbing knees
swirling water and air

whipping skin
then the off-balance

stomp
reel

a drunk dance
a child learning to walk

hope for the small miracle
of space

between stones
the slow ascent

into shallows
no baptism with this faith.

Deer in the Field

Two deer stand in the green March field
twitching noses, reading what news
travels the morning breeze

they bend to nibble fresh stalks of grass
yet alert to every fiber
of the empty space that surrounds them

tense rippling coats the color of dirt and wood
with spots of cloud. They are present
in the dawn. No memory of another day

glazes the black dwarf stars
of their eyes. They watch me move away,
the crackle of my thoughts sparking every step.

Man in Float Tube

from a photograph of Maurice Lartigue
by Jacques Henri Lartigue

It is the incongruity that draws the eye
to the jacket, hat and tie suspended there
above the water, snow on the rose,
the old man or woman curled in sleep
who suddenly resembles a child

and this carefully maintained air of formality.
One year later, April 15, 1912, fur coats
and sequined gowns, suits and a small field of fedoras gather
on the deck of *Titanic*, gazing out at the diamonds
reflecting moonlight on the still, black surface

as if what was so thoughtfully adorned, ritual of layer
upon layer, might add some buoyancy, hold one in place
over the ocean's dark miles.

And what of the water you find yourself treading?
All you fashion to remember your name?
Your finery soaks and grows heavy, draws the body down
and down, no matter how much you wave your arms.

It's your only choice: piece by sodden piece to pull
it off, let it fall away from you and sink,
swim back toward the light.

Dharma

This morning as I plant seeds in furrows
I marvel at what they grow into,
these nuggets packed with bushels of August
green beans, chips of corn that look as though they fell
off an ear and dried on the kitchen floor
under the stove growing into a city of stalks.
Dirt clods and stones tumble
down the sides against the seeds until I sweep
them away, then smooth the soil and hope for rain.
Sixty-foot oaks sleep inside the acorns
scattered on the grass.
Last month a robin
nested in the wreath on the front wall of the house,
roosting day after day with her beak agape
as if letting loose a long sigh. Soon four
downy drunken heads surfaced to check the view.
I was sure we should do something to prevent
them from falling, until one day, the nest empty
but for its down comforter, four robins
pecked at worms and danced the lawn, the same grass
that sprouts between the bricks I laid at the foot
of the stairs, no matter how hard I try to keep it out.

Dish Soap

When washing dishes, just wash dishes.
              —*Thich Nhat Hanh*

For a few weeks in May that old scrub lilac
blooms with the most delicate purple petals
and with others nearby fills the air with fragrance.
The cherry too with its wine colored sprigs
and the magnolia, each flower ready to string
into a garland. Then another spring storm
loses the flowers to the wind,
leaves growing out of cloudy green weather.
You might take this as a metaphor
for our lives, those few moments of radiance,
the months of drab routine but I am washing dishes,
smelling rain on the breeze.
Each plate sparkles,
the suds leave white blossoms on my hands.

Eliane Elias Plays Jobim

When she touches the keys
the piano sprinkles drops of water
over the audience. We hesitate

not sure we want to get wet,
our hair, clothes, what will we do
with ourselves and all the others watching?

Her dress hikes up her legs
the lightening flare
of her thighs pressed against the bench

as she bends over the keyboard
asking for more rain. She slips
off her shoes and pushes the pedals

with her bare feet, her eyes flashing—
she has seen these storms before,
in Brazil, and she laughs

shaking her head as we northerners
straight as corn rows
attempt to rein

in our desire
but the mist clings to us
despite ourselves, our shirts soak

through and under white linen
our bodies sway like flowers
in a shower, seeing through

ourselves and one another,
tossing our drenched hair,
splashing every puddle.

Lectio Divina @ Amazon.com

We understand
how the first warm breeze
after the long winter
reminded you of the dead
and the freedom you tasted
while peeing on the maple
and looking up at the stars

which is why we recommend
The Palm at the End of the Mind
by Wallace Stevens and the Upanishads.
People like you
have searched that sanctum sanctorum
of their rooms for a similar peace
that might dawn like sunlight
across the lake.
Some of them have read
the works of Thomas Merton and Thich Nhat Hanh.

You may have heard from Subaru
that your 120,000 mile service is due
in only 3,452 miles. In that case
you might enjoy *The Berkley to Boston
Forty Brick Lost Bag Blues, Auto Care
for Dummies*, and *The Best of Car Talk* cd.

Though we never witnessed you
kneeling at your bed asking for the inches
required to make the NBA or improve
your odds with girls

or watched you pocket
the Bazooka Joe bubblegum in the Kresges
or the economy size Velveeta
in the college Jewel years later

though we never saw you lift
the cracked old lady back to her feet
after she slipped on the ice patch
in the pharmacy parking lot

eight out of nine others found solace
in their prayers to the same God you petitioned

which is why we recommend
before heading to that final check out
you continue to visit your mother,
love your wife and children
and that toothless cursing stranger
who flipped you off when you smiled
to her at the store,
all those blooming flowers of moments,
so delicate, so soon gone.

Abandoned Farmhouse

The walls vanished board by board
on weekdays, so no one noticed
except the crows. The missing windows
offered a greater clarity,
the barn, its half-charred beams
and washed red planks caught
in their moment of collapse
might have cried out but had choked
on the words.
The long grass still outlined
a memory of lawn
until one day,
only a ring of stone remained,
a foundation housing
brown and green shards of broken glass
from beer bottles the delinquents
came to drink in the darkness
huddled out of the wind
behind the glow of cigarettes
that might emit just enough light
for them to recognize the shape
of the young woman floating on air
through the empty expanse of her kitchen,
singing some lost tune, stepping out back
through the silent swinging door to hang laundry
not seeming to notice
the sharpness of the wind or shrieking crows.

Another Morning

The tract mansion on the cul-de-sac,
skeletal wife and gifted children,
the buffed sheen of the profession
won't animate this morning
as you plod across the driveway
to your sparkling SUV.
Trees shushing in the cool wind,
cooing mourning doves, raucous crows,
the silver light on wet grass
and glimmer on the asphalt street
won't provide any newness to this day,
emerging from emptiness that isn't the past
so much as it is the darkness of sleep,
stillness an hour before dawn or birth.
You try to hold the world together
by the effort of your will,
friends who disappear into *Better Homes,*
parents slipping toward their burial plot for two.
It takes such concentration
to hold those 747s aloft over the city,
keep the cars in their lanes as they
surge the ribbons of freeways,
prevent the animals and children
from bolting. If you looked away
the universe itself could disappear,
the particles waiting for you
to call them into being.
Yet, each morning you wake and look around,
everything is right where you left it,
the dresser topped with loose change,
rumpled sheets scented with breath and skin,
even that memory of when, young enough
you saw some waves of brilliance
halo every bit of the world you entered,
the surging electric current
in the sandbox, in the tree house,
in the walks along the leafy streets
of delight.

The Servant of Small Things

Call me the servant of small things,
of the mongrel dog lying in cherry shade,
bone and bone and stick and mole
lined up before him as he tastes the wind,
watches lilac fade, sun seeping into fur
through the sashes of leaves

and of the cat in a square of sun
vibrating a mantra that space and time
aren't filled like a food bowl or cup
of Milky Way, silence overflowing silence,
pouring over the rim of morning,
puddling on the lawn.

In seven languages the birds call out their names
or yours or mine as I pour sunflower seeds into feeders.
Some of them are Brazilian
jazz singers who touch your skin with their voices

as the maple dances in its robe of Canadian flags,
the dogwood wears its white shawl all May.
But this is a sultry summer song
so the willow in her grass skirt
sways a slow hula each time the wind blows,
whispering certain words of love
that only a servant of small things can hear.

Share

During the night something has slid out from the shadows of the pines and eaten the leaves off four rows of green beans. In the morning nothing left but columns of stem spikes as if I were looking down from a plane at telephone poles along the road. Three times I replant. Three times when the first two delicate leaves unfurl they never see morning sun. There are the usual suspects. Deer that float through pre-dawn mist then vaporize in the trees before light comes. Raccoons will eat anything, using their little human hands to open bird feeders or slurp down a suet cake they have lifted from its cage. For bean leaves, the rabbits. I see a few even in the naked light of mid-day, looking fat and nervous. "You have to share with the animals," my naturalist friend chuckles. "Share with the animals," my wife insists as I consider a chicken wire or electric fence penitentiary. But I do share, even that morning when I find the severed stalk on my rose bush, and gone, the one red bloom, gone with the animals to that dark, mysterious night table where with my plants and rose, they gather listening to the cicadas shake maracas, and the crickets pull their bows.

Color of Weather

On the television weather radar
this morning, the land of Southwest Michigan
is painted with a swath of blue
that lies above a thick brush stroke of pink
atop a lawn of green that sprouts
from northern Indiana all the way to Kalamazoo.
But when the dogs and I greet
the chill morning air opening the door
and emerging into the out-of-doors
to start our daily walk there is only sleet falling
cold clear pebbles spraying the ground and road.

The Heaven of Dogs

You might have heard
they wait at the end
of a rainbow bridge
for their owners to join them
but that is a human version
of their heaven.

In the heaven of dogs
they run unleashed
through wildflower fields

chasing groundhogs
they flip into the air
like frisbees

and drive their own cars
to the Milkbone Mart.
Yes, they hang their heads
out the window.

In their dreams
they float and fall
through clouds
with their friends, the cats,
splashing in the grass
so everything grows.

A day is just a day
as it was in their lives on earth,
a single moment passing,
each drop of time holding all
of time, a nap, a long stretch,
breath of lilac in the breeze,
just *this*.

Waking

Waking from a dream to this present rain.
The oily darkness, flash of blue lightning
in the west over the cornfield.
Before dawn, the air drips mystery,
as if a dream bleeds out into space.
The storm approaches—soft touch of a breeze
on the wind chimes.
Certain birds stir the pines.
The boughs nod up and down.
The dogs twitch their paws and whimper
in their sleep.
If I looked into the mirror
I might not recognize myself.

Six A.M.

It is raining lightly in the dark
thunder in the distant west
as the grumbling night
wanders off to its bedroom
turning out the lights as it goes
while from the east dawn approaches
flicking them all on again
one by one
along the corridor of morning

Zazen

Open a pair of lace curtains
in the living room

of an old country home
surrounded by nothing but miles

of cornfields
and a lake that no one ever named

the yellow sun staining
the white fabric

and all the words
you might have once called upon

sparking the air
like specks of dust

Mourning Doves

They are gathering again on the long pews
of the telephone wire outside my bedroom
window to remind me I suppose
that somewhere someone grieves.
They offer their single low note
that embodies pain and tenderness,
a cooing that contains within it
the moan that accompanies all we love
falling away over time
though even while their smooth brown
and white feathers let fall on the ground
a shadow larger than themselves
chickadees and sparrows veer and coast below them
to the feeder and then quickly to the trees
singing notes that sound like laughter.

Rain

I was going to get up but then it started to rain.
I could hear it whispering something to the leaves

and ringing a wind chime though nothing more
than a slight breeze accompanied the rain.

The dogs were sleeping on the carpet.
They were listening to the rain with their eyes closed.

The crickets stopped rubbing their itchy legs.
Some birds gargled in the pines.

All the flowers lowered their heads for the moment
the way people do at a service when they examine

their shoes and wonder how they will ever get
from here to there without getting soaking wet in the rain.

Country Poem

The young boy is waiting
for the girl to outgrow her love of horses,
all that heat and flesh against blue jean legs.

She clatters off once again in the afternoon,
following the long dirt road that snakes
between the hills. The father watches her

disappear over the rise, the sun floating
on the green ocean of fields.
He knows he has bought

only a little time.
The boy will return
like a coyote in the night,

tossing a handful of gravel
at the bedroom window
until one morning the curtains

billowing like white gowns
from the breeze entering the empty room.
Some Sunday,

the baby wrapped in a blanket,
husband following with saddle bags
of supplies, she'll never ask

about former loves, he'll never tell her
about that day or where in the field
he dug the pit with his tractor.

Drink

Annie Regend drank turpentine
she had to have her stomach pumped

we all ran home

Markie couldn't come out to play

Father insisted they take certain seats
at the dinner table

green crystal goblets filled
with warm milk

Mother wanted that bottle of vodka
she bought at Oxford Beverage
on the way home from the park

we were sitting on towels
in the back seat still wet from the pool

we waited in the car watched her open
the brown bag so the neck of the pint
stuck out she twisted off the plastic cap

and crouching almost to the seat
took a swig that bubbled the bottle
a gulp that must have painted the blue
back into the sky it must have been that good

the sun burned the hood the air dancing
with waves of heat how she must have waited

her will coiled like a spring as we screamed
and dunked each other in the water

all afternoon how that drink must have felt
to her like a sacrament like communion.

Walking

A darkness joins me each day
out into the fields, past the ponds and along the swamp.
It leaves me in the cool, thick pines
then returns on the dirt road next to the corn field.
I've become as quiet as this darkness,
silent as the sunlight pouring over the field.
The weed and I understand each other.
The lone tree in the middle of the eighty acres,
that's me.
I love the mornings and the evenings,
the edges of light and shadow,
how the trees become charcoal drawings
on the pale paper of the sky,
the bee balm and lavender bloom of clouds behind them,
how the silence pools at the base
of trees, exhales the suggestion of night
into the air where six geese etch a line
across the empty sky.

Horde

In such dry heat, a crack between slabs of rough-sawn siding and a hole in the lawn out by the garden became fountains that sprayed bees instead of water droplets. They veered all directions of some mysterious service. I had wanted to just let them be until one afternoon when I mowed grass they swarmed, stinging my face, arms, legs, ankles, dozens of relentless injections swelling into allergic nausea as I slapped at them and ran, yelled to my wife and daughter to get into the house. I came back with a can of Black Flag, crept up to the humming crevice in the wall that disappeared into its own shadow and sprayed, sprayed, sprayed, sprayed until the crack dripped like a faucet and I breathed the sweet odor of poison. Then with a gas can to the hole dug out in the grass I poured it full, lit a match and dropped it in, stepping back for the explosion, the sting of heat wiping my face, crackling black smoke puffing from its mouth. I killed them all and turned to the house where my wife and daughter stood behind the window. I was alone listening to the silence, that buzz the ears make when there is no sound.

Moths on the Screen

Yes, there was the hush of light rain
and when the rain ended the sighs
of distant birds.

There may have been a whisper of grass
beginning to grow again after a month of sun

an almost imperceptible exhalation like the light winds
that come from a mayfly twitching its wings

not enough to move the silver pipes of the wind chime
or pull a leaf from its stem

just a suggestion of breath
like the presence of animals that edge
at dawn and dusk from the trees
to the rim of the cornfields

or those who in our silence
visit us though far away or long dead.

Swimming After Labor Day

They've disassembled the dock
and stacked it under a blue tarp.

Plywood boards lid the windows
of the concession stand. The trash cans
no longer cough napkins into the wind.

Only gulls remain, soaring like lost silver kites
along the shoreline, calling out to the gusts
that flap the shredded flag.

Waves rushing sand
keeping time the old way
water charged with autumn
as I walk out into the deepening blue
breathe in the cold air and dive.

Dead Letter

He had wanted to be a mail carrier
but not a teacher.

Each day, hour by hour,
as he delivered what he would insist

was his third-class lecture, he watched
the slots of his students' eyes slowly close,

the empty boxes of their mouths drop open.
He had nothing for them today

no correspondence or note they might keep
pressed between the pages of a yearbook

in that heavy bag of obligations
he shouldered to school each morning.

Relapse

Your bad habits come back to visit like old college friends. It can only be a short stay, they insist, only a day or two, perhaps a long weekend before they must get back to the family, to their responsibilities, to their hard-won prosperity. They've changed too, they tell you, and understand your reluctance to revisit those wild days on the campus of the Seven Sins. *When you live in the present, there's no such thing as a one-night stand*, one chuckles, offering a silver butane lighter that clicks open and closed like a lock. And, yes, you can feel your youth return, shinnying up your spine, offering a certain clarity to your eyes as if intelligence could be unwrapped from the gauze of time. *One should celebrate life by swallowing it*, another says, winking. And before you know it, they are unpacking their smelly suitcases in the guest room, never complaining that you woke them too early with the hacking cough you seem recently to have developed. While you're in the shower scrubbing yourself in the steam, you plot the ways you will get them to leave.

The Mouse Above My Daughter's Bedroom Ceiling

Stench descending thick as fog,
unmistakable emanation of decay

I had smelled before when I had forgotten
to check the traps a few weeks straight

at the end of fall when every year it seemed
the mice found a way into our house.

There were no traps above her room,
unreachable from the rafters

that blocked the way, so I assumed
it must have died from some natural cause

and fallen still in this protected place.
Though we sprayed and ran the ceiling fan

that rancid odor wouldn't dissipate
until finally I considered cutting

through the drywall with a saw,
ripping out a piece of the ceiling

to get to where that lump of fur
slowly melted into a dust pile,

anything to move that smell
once and for all out of our lives

until one day it finally disappeared
the fall my brother died.

Leaves, Turning

What is personality but an endless
set of rehearsals?
                    —*Jim Harrison*

The trees by the road have begun to turn.
The summer sunlight that once sustained them
lost its touch and finally disappeared
from cold mornings until the leaves became
in its absence astounding: blood red oak,
rusty elm, golden poplar returning
to the color of their nature the way
people sometimes do, who might shine one day
with a genuine honesty and it
is then you can love them the way you fall
in love with October, seeing the land
set afire, saying to yourself it has
been this way all along, the way beauty
so often is, covered, lying within.

Before Dusk

It may have been the way everything
turned honey-colored for that hour
of afternoon October sun

when the low clouds separated
to let in a new light catching the rain
and mist before they disappeared

the maple leaves were golden shivers
in the breeze some tumbling along the street
toward gullies and ditches

the fields of corn hadn't yet been harvested
the corn leaves waving each gust of wind
as the long weeds lifted their yellow skirts and danced

that made me think wherever
this season is heading it must be beautiful
as evening when the sun

sets behind the cornfield
and the tree limbs grow stark and black
as the crows that follow one another

across the field following the light.

Early October Snow

It will not stay.
But this morning we wake to pale muslin
stretched across the grass.
The pumpkins, still in the fields, are planets
shrouded by clouds.
The Weber wears a dunce cap
and sits in the corner by the garage
where asters wrap scarves
around their necks to warm their blooms.
The leaves, still soldered to their branches
by a frozen drop of dew, splash
apple and pear paint along the roadsides.
It seems we have glanced out a window
into the near future, mid-December, say,
the black and white photo of winter
carefully laid over the present autumn,
like a morning we pause at the mirror
inspecting the single strand of hair
that overnight has turned to snow.

Four Haibun in November

I

Walking with the dogs up the hill to the clover field, the wind carving our faces, cold and brisk, the dogs sniffing, alert, as they trot the dirt road. An empty plastic grocery bag clings to a sumac branch. The leaves have blown away, except for a few trees on the north side of the woods still yellow with autumn. The flannel fall has come to an end, Indian Summer with its palette of red, gold, bronze, yellow and orange, with its corn stalks bundled with wire, blocks of stacked straw, gourds and pumpkins to make into soups and rattles. Now dusk lasts all day, the steady rain changes to sleet, to snow, and back again to rain. The spindles of bare branches in the woods like the quills of porcupines. Late fall begins.

> The November wind
> Has erased all the color
> From the autumn trees

II

This is the most quiet day in November, more quiet than a few days ago when no matter where you stood, in the empty field littered with strands of corn leaves, in the woods where the rain from last week still puddled in the lowlands, a distant bugle played notes carried on the wind from the veterans cemetery, and they replaced the bird songs that trembled the pines. Now the feeders hanging on cables outside the window sway to and fro like chapel bells only because of the cold November wind, the perches all empty, sunflower seeds gone, the birds off to where grass still grows, and we, in this northern place, listening to wind, knowing the firearm season begins before the first light of dawn.

> The leaves scurry off
> Like herds of small animals
> Moving toward winter

III

The snow is gathering light from the moon, from the vapor light across the field by the barn, from the aluminum gutters and the surface of the lake. The snow that fell all day yesterday, Lake Michigan transformed into a flurry, made the day undefined, slick, steamy. Cars crawled the roads and then disappeared for good. This is a dark time. What will we do? Surrounded by darkness, yet the snow is gathering light. If you walk this morning before dawn, you will see well enough to know your way.

> The moonlight pieces
> Diced in the snowy field
> Are only one moon

IV

It was raining. The fields had been harvested. Now they were brown scalps under a gray cloud. Then there was a lightening, a hint of silver in the sky, streak of sunshine. The raindrops swelled and turned white and feathery in the wind. It was as if a cocoon had burst open and white butterflies had appeared. Or a blanket hatch of September mayflies had erupted on the river. Snowflakes rising and falling, veering in every direction. The field slowly turned white. The trees along the road turned white. The deer hunters couldn't see and left for home to dry out, and the deer moved to the edge of the trees to look out at the field and the snow.

Rain changing to snow
A pick-up truck passed by
Tracks already gone

Written in November After Cold Winds Have Torn the Trees Bare

Autumn sunset,
rose and lilac.

Late Fall

Yesterday the trees sprinkled leaves
           along the path in the November woods
               and once from a gust the leaves
         under an oak swirled upward
and became a flock of sparrows

IV

Winter Morning

Here in winter the testament
to what is holy:

rumpled sheets of snow
gathering silver moonlight

the ink webwork of trees
crow caws piercing the hint of sunrise.

In the columns of chimney smoke
in the white stream of breath

in the snake trail of footsteps
crossing the drifts

as the gold threads of dawn
ignite the distances.

Thaw

That one day of December rain
washes away the forgetful snow

moldering leaves still freckling the grass
unvarnished deck boards, side roads

with big gulps and beer cans winking
gold and silver like false teeth

in the sudden sunshine.
How easy it is to recall one by one

those venial sins and inadequacies
of long ago that for so many years

lay hidden somewhere within
the ashen mounds of the brain.

Ahimsa

I don't want to kill the mice that came in looking for a bit of warmth in the winter and then got hungry and decided to look for a snack in the cereal cabinets. I want to live without harming, let them live their twitching whiskered lives. But I don't want to live with them either, shitting in the pantry, in the drawers where the silverware is stacked in plastic dividers, in the cupboards with the Rice Krispies and Quaker Oats. When they take up residence in the woodpile outside I might even choose some further logs not to ruin their work. When they cruise the sills in the barn I go about my business of oil and machinery. I might catch them in live traps and release them somewhere, maybe after a long drive, blindfolded, but they always return and more of them. I know they will breed, and can hear them as they take over every dark crevice behind the walls, above the ceiling, munching the insulation and wiring to weave it into bedding for their dark nests.

A Beautiful Snowy Day

What if all we wish
we had said in our lives

began descending from the clouds
as snow, each flake "I love you"

from that sullen neighbor boy
kicking an ice chunk down the road

that fell from the wheel well
of a passing car, flakes whispering

"hold me," "I have tried," as the widow
dries the one plate and places it back

in the cupboard, as the driver pulls
the gas gun from the pump at the station,

snow spiraling toward the streets
and fields which are filling now

with a certain softness as the swirling
hushes and sighs in what might have been

a wind but is instead the breath
of mothers, fathers, friends, spouses

partners, sisters, brothers, so many
who are waking from a dream

in which they could not speak, a dream
in which their mouths were frozen closed

and all they could do was look around
at the snow and go on with their baffling, silent lives.

Walnuts in Winter

The squirrel's brain is approximately the size of a walnut.

In this snow-covered field
with the grass and the ponds
shining and rime crusted the deer

and the rabbits somehow understand
that in the orange days of October
the walnut trees scattered nuts

around their trunks and that they
still lie there under the snow
waiting to be pawed free

chomped and broken open
the soft heart chewed and swallowed
though they will not reach those

under the plate of frozen ground
that the squirrels buried
as they scuttled around here

all autumn, storing food and perhaps
with a joy we have yet to understand
at such abundance planting walnut trees.

To a Coyote

The farmers despise your kind I'm told
because you favor the nutrient-rich organs
of lambs that you devour without first killing them

and I imagine the bloodstained fur
around your pale tan mouth, black lips
and even teeth dangling a few scraps

of flesh when I find you on the side
of the road, lying across some fallen tree trunks
and branches that hold you above the ground

your body bent back on itself
and your head twisted toward the road.
The hunters who searched for you

with their pick-up trucks and walkie-talkies
all winter never found you. I had hoped
they wouldn't each morning I saw them

when I was out walking my dogs.
There is no blood anywhere
on your golden and white fur

still trembling a little in the breeze,
no gunshot wound or arrow puncture.
Your purple tongue hangs out

as if you might open your eyes
and lick my hand as I lift you
off the logs to place you on the ground

out of sight of the road
while the snow slowly falls over us both
over the woods, over the road

covering your body with its cool blanket
covering my tracks as I slip back up the road
unseen in the gathering morning light.

Old Man River

I sing most mornings in the shower,
in the garage gathering firewood
for the stove, usually Beatles ballads
like "Norwegian Wood," or "Since I Fell
for You" the way Al Jarreau did it,
Sinatra, "That's Life," and, sometimes I admit,
Tom Jones, "It's Not Unusual"

all in my narrow middle range
except for that morning I wake,
my head congested,
my voice croaking an octave above
the inaudible hum of the universe.
Then for a short while
I am one of the basses

and while starting a pot of coffee
launch into "Old Man River,"
a song I do only when suffering as I am now,
a certain power vibrating
the tight muscles of my chest,
deep moan of the Mississippi,
Jules Bledsoe and Paul Robeson.

You an' me, we sweat an' strain
Body all achin' and wracked wid pain
Tote dat barge! Lift dat bale!
Git a little drunk and ya lands in jail

I sing all the way out the door
into the bruised darkness of this January morning
to sweep snow off my daughter's car
while she dries her hair.

After the Ice Storm

I heard a rock shatter the window
of the sky.

Broken glass was falling,
rattling the roofs,
shaking the light from the trees.

Now all the woods have turned to glass;
the branches, tinkling chandeliers.
The pines wear shawls of diamonds

around their shoulders.
The crystal stems gather every color.
Limbs litter the roads.

How are we to hold this fragile world?

In Winter

Last night when blue moonlight
glazed the snow I watched

a shooting star streak across the sky
its startling silence in the breath-clouded air

and thought for a moment perhaps yes
that could be you but how

when perched on a rafter in the barn
the owl suddenly shivers its feathers

how when the red-tailed hawk
glides above the field in the dark?

In February

Now even the cardinals

those blood spatters

have disappeared

and only the crows are left

solemn in their black suits

pulling a shroud

over the field's stiff face.

Firewood

In fall, we were rich with firewood
and stacked our abundance by the cord
in the shade under the pines,
pulling a tarp over the top of each row
to keep it dry from November rains
and later the snows.

Now, almost February, mornings
hairy with frost and locked in ice,
the wood pile shrinks with startling speed
each cold week, the empty space around it
expands and fills with air

as we bang our shoes toward March
and the equinox, hoping for a spell
of mild weather, hoping what remains will last

occasionally marching out the back door
with a can full of ashes
to dump in the tall, stiff weeds.

Assimilation

When the Virgin of Guadalupe first appeared on their sliding glass door, she looked like frost that wouldn't melt when the morning sun streamed through her robe, and she gleamed each night from the stars with the darkness behind her. The door would have been better suited to a home down south, uninsulated metal frames that grew thick rinds of ice all winter, glued hands that tried to force it open, fingers stuck like tongues on a school-yard fence. For awhile, they accepted the inconvenience of her in their lives, used a blow dryer each morning to let out the dog, swept the rose petals scattered across the kitchen floor. At parties, guests posed with her for photographs. They considered leaking her to the media, sure that wishful believers would gather in the backyard, ready to pony up to see her, even if from behind, but eventually she just made their lives too difficult, too much work to step out into the world each day, so they bought a new door with e argon sealed glass and a maple sash, and when the workmen took her away, one on each arm, she looked like one of the nuns they arrest for standing for peace.

Let Snow Fall

after Jane Kenyon

Let snow fall
over fields, over country roads.

Let snow sugar the pine boughs,
the black limbs and branch thickets
of the forests.

Let snow fill city streets, boulevards,
driveways, parking lots,

heap upon the rooftops
of Washington, Kabul, Baghdad, Tel Aviv.

Let drifts close every school
and office, let phones ring
unanswered in the ministries.

Let snow urge us
back to those we love,
back into our homes

where chimneys pipe clouds
into our blue sky
over the whole, quiet planet.

More Snow

This morning, heavy snow, limb-
bending snow, bough-breaking
branch-snapping snow.

The pines are tired old women
carrying their laundry

hauling the folded and stacked
months of winter toward the March thaw

white sheets and towels
that the wind spills into the fields.

Black Ice

Those with the greatest faith
in Goodyear or four-wheel drive
stand shivering, blowing into their cupped hands
beside their cars where the ditch becomes a front
lawn or cornfield.

The asphalt is a glass pipe
that disappears into a tunnel of trees. It's bound
to be even worse down there, we say
huddled in the red glow of taillights and exhaust
our small town meeting of those
who stopped to see if the slide-offs were okay

as another car slows and slows
then lurches toward work,
only a firm grip on the wheel and hope
holding the tires to the road.

About the Author

Robert Haight was born in Detroit and educated at Michigan State University and Western Michigan University, where he received a B.A. in English and an M.F.A. in Creative Writing. He has published two poetry collections, *Water Music* and *Emergences and Spinner Falls*, and he has written essays and articles on fly fishing, the environment, education and spirituality for a variety of edited books, journals and magazines. His writing has won awards from the Poetry Resource Center of Michigan, Western Michigan University, the Kalamazoo Foundation and the Arts Foundation of Michigan. He teaches writing, literature and meditation at Kalamazoo Valley Community College and lives at Hemlock Lake in Cass County, Michigan.

Other Recent Titles from Mayapple Press: